Saint Bernards

By Maria Nelson

Gareth Stevens
Publishing

Please visit our website, www.garethstevens.com. For a free color catalog of all our high-quality books, call toll free 1-800-542-2595 or fax 1-877-542-2596.

Library of Congress Cataloging-in-Publication Data

Nelson, Maria.
  Saint Bernards / Maria Nelson.
     p. cm. — (Great big dogs)
  Includes index.
  ISBN 978-1-4339-5792-5 (pbk.)
  ISBN 978-1-4339-5793-2 (6-pack)
  ISBN 978-1-4339-5790-1 (library binding)
  1. Saint Bernard dog—Juvenile literature. I. Title.
  SF429.S3N45 2011
  636.73—dc22

                                        2010046766

First Edition

Published in 2012 by
Gareth Stevens Publishing
111 East 14th Street, Suite 349
New York, NY 10003

Copyright © 2012 Gareth Stevens Publishing

Designer: Andrea Davison-Bartolotta
Editor: Kristen Rajczak

Photo credits: Cover, pp. 1, 5, 6, 14 Shutterstock.com; p. 9 Thomas J. Abercrombie/National Geographic/Getty Images; p. 10 iStockphoto/Thinkstock; pp. 13, 20 iStockphoto.com; p. 17 Justin Pumfrey/Taxi/Getty Images; p. 18 Doug Pensinger/Getty Images.

Printed in the United States of America

CPSIA compliance information: Batch #CS11GS: For further information contact Gareth Stevens, New York, New York at 1-800-542-2595.

Contents

Beautiful Saint Bernards 4

Story of a Saint 7

Barry Dogs 8

Long or Short? 11

Red Rover 12

Big Paws, Big Dogs 15

Living Like a Saint 16

Famous Saints 19

Owning a Saint Bernard 20

Glossary 22

For More Information 23

Index 24

Words in the glossary appear in **bold** type the first time they are used in the text.

Beautiful Saint Bernards

Saint Bernards are some of the most beautiful dogs around! They're large and have brightly colored coats and friendly features.

The Saint Bernard **breed** grew from dogs the Roman armies brought to Switzerland almost 2,000 years ago. They worked as guards and herders near a mountain range called the Swiss Alps. They were sometimes called Alpine **mastiffs**, mountain dogs, or Swiss Alpine dogs. The American Kennel Club recognized the Saint Bernard breed in 1885.

Saint Bernards have a rich history.

Dog Tales

A Roman Catholic pope made Bernard de Menthon a saint in 1681.

These Saint Bernards are ready for the cold weather in the Swiss Alps!

Story of a Saint

Saint Bernard dogs are named after a Catholic saint. Bernard de Menthon was a **priest**. By 1050, he had founded two **hospices** in the Alps between Switzerland and Italy. Travelers rested and waited out snowstorms there. Two unsafe mountain paths were named in honor of him—the Great St. Bernard pass and the Little St. Bernard pass.

Monks took over the hospices. They used dogs to find travelers lost in the snow.

7

Barry Dogs

The monks' "hospice dogs" helped save many people who became lost while traveling through the mountains. The dogs' great sense of smell helped the monks find people in the snow. The most famous of these dogs was named Barry. Barry saved about 40 people in the mountains during the early 1800s. The hospice dogs were sometimes called "Barry dogs" in his honor.

The monks' dogs became well known all over the world. They were the beginning of the modern Saint Bernard breed.

Dog Tales

In 1815, Barry's body was put on display at the Natural History Museum in Switzerland. It's still there today.

This Saint Bernard is being trained by a monk.

9

Long-haired Saint Bernards are more recognizable to dog owners in the United States.

Long or Short?

Saint Bernards can have short hair or long hair. A short-haired Saint is "smooth coated." A long-haired Saint is "rough coated," but it's still soft to touch. The Saint Bernards at the Swiss hospices had short hair at first. The monks used long-haired dogs to create Saint Bernards with longer hair. They thought the dogs would be warmer when working in the snow. Instead, ice formed on the long-haired Saints' coats. The ice made it harder for the dogs to work.

Red Rover

Saint Bernards' coats are usually white and red. The red can look brownish or brownish yellow. Parts of their coats can also be **brindle** or black. Both long-haired and short-haired Saints **shed**, but the long-haired dogs shed more.

Saint Bernards have black fur around their eyes, nose, and ears that's called a "mask." The mask looks different on each dog. Some dogs' whole faces are black. Some only have black around one eye.

Saint Bernards have white fur on their faces, feet, chests, and the tips of their tails.

13

Dog Tales

Seeing a Saint Bernard puppy's parents is a good way to tell about how big the puppy will be as an adult.

Saint Bernards are fully grown at 2 or 3 years old.

Big Paws, Big Dogs

Saint Bernard puppies only weigh a few pounds when they're born. By the time they're a few months old, they have huge paws! Saint Bernards have no problem growing into their paws. As adults, they are usually 25 to 27 inches (64 to 69 cm) tall at the shoulder and weigh a lot! Saints can be 110 to 200 pounds (50 to 91 kg). Saint Bernards also have loose black lips and a large head with a wide face.

Living Like a Saint

Saint Bernards are very independent dogs. They're smart and can be trained easily. But they also like to make their own rules! Saints don't need a lot of exercise. Sometimes, they won't want any. It's important to take them outside and go for walks.

Saints make good watchdogs. They're faithful **protectors** of their family and home. Saints' bark and size may scare people who don't know them. However, they're usually friendly dogs.

Dog Tales

Saints like to play, but not when it's hot outside. Saints need a lot of water and a cool place to nap when they're hot.

Saint Bernards are gentle with young children.

17

Dog Tales

Several colleges have a Saint Bernard as their **mascot**.

This photo is from Bernie's first Avalanche game.

▷

Famous Saints

The Colorado Avalanche hockey team's mascot is a Saint Bernard named Bernie. Bernie became the mascot in 2009. He wears a number 1 shaped like a bone.

One of the most famous Saint Bernards is Beethoven. This lovable dog starred in six movies. The first movie, *Beethoven*, came out in 1992.

Nana, the dog in the Disney movie *Peter Pan*, is also a Saint Bernard. However, Nana is a Newfoundland in the play on which the movie is based.

Owning a Saint Bernard

Saint Bernards are not easy dogs to own. They can get into trouble easily because they're big and adventurous. Saints are strong and can be hard to control. They should be trained before they get too big to handle.

Saints all drool—and some drool a lot. Still, Saint Bernards are a loving part of many families. Well-trained Saints will protect their owners and welcome new friends!

Learning About Saint Bernards

height	25 to 27 inches (64 to 69 cm) at the shoulder
weight	110 to 200 pounds (50 to 91 kg)
coloring	white and red or reddish brown with a black mask
life span	8 to 10 years

Glossary

breed: a group of animals that share features different from other groups of the kind

brindle: uneven dark bands on lighter-colored fur

hospice: a place for travelers to stay

mascot: a person, animal, or thing that is the sign of a group

mastiff: a large, powerful dog

monk: a man who gives up everything for his faith and lives with others like him

priest: a person who leads church services of a certain faith

protector: one who keeps others safe

shed: to lose fur

Books

Hall, Lynn. *Barry: The Bravest Saint Bernard*. New York, NY:
Paw Prints, 2008.

Salzmann, Mary Elizabeth. *Super Saint Bernards*. Edina, MN:
ABDO Publishing Company, 2011.

Websites

Bernie the Saint Bernard
www.berniethemascot.com
Find out more about the Colorado Avalanche's mascot.

Saint Bernard Club of America
www.saintbernardclub.org
Learn more about Saint Bernards.

Index

Alpine mastiffs 4

American Kennel Club 4

Barry 8, 9

Barry dogs 8

Beethoven 19

Beethoven 19

Bernard de Menthon 6, 7

Bernie 18, 19

breed 4, 8

coats 4, 11, 12

colors 4, 12, 13, 21

drool 20

exercise 16

hospices 7, 8, 11

life span 21

long-haired 10, 11, 12

mask 12, 21

monks 7, 8, 9, 11

mountain dogs 4

Nana 19

Peter Pan 19

protectors 16, 20

puppies 14, 15

rough coated 11

short-haired 11, 12

smooth coated 11

Swiss Alpine dogs 4

Swiss Alps 4, 6, 7

Switzerland 4, 7, 9

training 9, 16, 20

travelers 7, 8

watchdogs 16